MASTER

Your Feelings

They colour our perceptions, shape our experiences,
and influence our behaviours!

Harrison S. Mungal, Ph.D, Psy.D

Master Your Feelings

Contact author via email: info@harrisonmungal.com

info@agetoage.ca

www.agetoage.ca

www.harrisonmungal.com

www.harrisonmungalbooks.com

Facebook: Harrison Mungal

Twitter: AgeToAgeInc1

LinkedIn: Harrison Mungal, Ph.D., PsyD

YouTube: Harrison Mungal

Phone: 905-533-1334

ABOUT *the* AUTHOR

Harrison Sharma Mungal, BTh, MCC, MSW, PhD, PsyD

Harrison Sharma Mungal, possessing dual doctoral distinctions in Clinical Psychology and Philosophy in Social Work, demonstrates an unwavering commitment to ameliorating the well-being of his clients. Renowned internationally for his profound insights into cognitive therapy, his expertise spans mental health, addiction, relationships, and family dynamics.

In his role as a highly sought-after workshop presenter, Dr. Mungal extends his practical approach to assisting individuals, couples, families, and corporations. His global influence is evident through engaging presentations at conferences, seminars, and media platforms, where he adeptly integrates humor and enthusiasm into nuanced discussions on mental health, addiction, relationships, and parenting.

Dr. Mungal's innovative and scientifically grounded methodology has garnered acclaim, earning him accolades from diverse institutions. He extends his influence through offering training and consultations to a wide array of community partners, including esteemed professionals in the medical, social work, first responder, law enforcement, and senior management domains.

Actively involved in pioneering cognitive research, Dr. Mungal leads ground-breaking studies addressing mental health challenges such as addiction, psychosis, anxiety, and depression. His work includes the exploration of practical applications, exemplified by initiatives like music therapy for schizophrenia, substance abuse and addictions in the food service industry, and vaccination protocols for young children.

With over two decades of professional acumen, Dr. Mungal has left an indelible mark on the fields of mental health and psychiatry, providing services to diverse communities impacted by brain injuries, refugees, victims of warfare, and individuals in crisis. His pragmatic therapeutic repertoire encompasses evidence-based treatments like Cognitive Behavioural Therapy (CBT), Cognitive Processing Therapy (CPT), Dialectical Behavioural Therapy (DBT), Thought Developmental Practice (TDP) and Acceptance and Commitment Therapy (ACT).

TABLE *of* CONTENT

INTRODUCTION

In the journey of personal development, mastering one's feelings is a pivotal aspect that often dictates the course of our lives. Our thoughts, intertwined with our emotions, can either propel us forward or hold us back. Within the chapters of this exploration, we delve into the realm of mental toughness and the cultivation of a positive mindset, both crucial elements in mastering our feelings.

In this booklet we unravel the intricate relationship between our thoughts and emotions which affects our feelings. By understanding how our thoughts shape our feelings, we gain insight into the power of cognitive reframing and rational thinking. Through practical exercises and cognitive-behavioral techniques, we learn to harness the strength of our thoughts to navigate the complexities of our emotional landscape.

Mastering our feelings requires a deliberate effort to gain control over our emotional responses. By honing our self-awareness and self-regulation skills, we empower ourselves to navigate life's challenges with grace and composure.

With a resilient mindset, we embrace challenges as opportunities for growth and transformation, rather than obstacles to be feared.

A positive mindset is the cornerstone of emotional well-being and success. By fostering optimism, gratitude, and self-belief, we shift our perspective from one of scarcity to one of abundance. Through the cultivation of positive affirmations and visualization techniques, we rewire our brains for positivity and possibility. This helps to embrace positive feelings and condition our minds to think optimistic. With a resilient mindset and a positive outlook, we approach life's trials and triumphs with unwavering confidence and optimism.

In the pages that follow, we embark on a journey of self-discovery and empowerment, uncovering the tools and strategies needed to master our feelings, develop mental toughness, and cultivate a positive mindset. Together, let us embark on this transformative quest towards emotional mastery and personal fulfillment.

THOUGHTS *and not*
FEELINGS

Thoughts and feelings work together. This matters in our daily lives. It changes how we make choices and get along with others. Since they matter so much, we should understand how they work together. Feelings can be reacting to perceptions which can create several ongoing psychological issues. You could feel afraid of an animal, but that do not mean the animal will hurt you. Factual Information is necessary to help feelings and thoughts.

The difference between thoughts and feelings may seem small, but understanding this basic difference has a big impact on our mental health. Thoughts are cognitive and can be expressed clearly in words. They may be the result of reasoning and can often be categorized as facts or opinions.

For example, "I need to finish this project by tomorrow" is a thought based on a specific situation and a real deadline.

Feelings, on the other hand, are emotional reactions that may not necessarily be grounded in rational thought. They are our internal responses that show up physically and emotionally. For instance, you might feel stressed about the project mentioned above. That stress is not a thought; it's an emotional state that comes from our thoughts and possibly other factors like past experiences, our natural tendency towards work, and even our current physical state like sleep quality or general health.

Understanding the difference can lead to more effective emotional control. By labeling experiences accurately as thoughts or feelings, we can better manage our reactions to different situations. This difference can guide our coping strategies. If we're dealing with a negative thought, we might counter it with factual evidence. Managing a feeling might involve physical activities like deep breathing or going for a walk.

Overthinking can take over and cause anxiety and stress. It happens when we dwell too much on decisions, issues, or fears. This gets in the way of handling life and work well. Overthinking can happen in personal or professional situations. It often leads to being unable to act because we may fear all the possible outcomes too much.

There are ways to address overthinking. One effective strategy is mindfulness. This involves focusing on the present moment without judgment. Mindfulness practices like deep breathing, grounding exercises, or meditation can stop the cycle of overthinking. They draw our attention away from the looping thoughts and into the here and now.

Another approach is cognitive restructuring. This cognitive-behavioural technique identifies and challenges the irrational thinking and distortions that fuel overthinking. We can ask ourselves questions to challenge our thoughts, like "Is this based on facts?" or "What's the worst that could happen, and could I handle it?" By addressing overthinking, we gain control of our thoughts and reduce the stress and anxiety that come with them.

Understanding the difference between thoughts and feelings is vital. So is knowing how to manage feelings. These skills help achieve balance and well-being. Whether it's telling apart emotions and thinking or using mindfulness to stop constant worrying, the insights we gain are invaluable life tools.

Not all thoughts are equal. Some thoughts happen quickly, without thinking them through. These fast, instinctive thoughts can lead to hasty choices or words we later regret. Other thoughts are well thought-out after careful thinking and reflection.

Fast thoughts aren't always bad. They can lead to honest, candid reactions when we need to decide or respond quickly. But they can also lead to mistakes or hurtful comments without thinking first. Well thought-out thoughts let us better understand situations. This makes it more likely our actions or decisions will be good in the long run.

To manage these different thoughts effectively, it's essential to recognize when they happen. In emotional or fast-moving situations, take a brief pause to think. Even a few seconds can change a fast thought into a more thought-out one. This can make our actions and interactions more positive.

Managing our thoughts and feelings is an important skill. Realizing that our thoughts don't have to control our feelings is a big step. Just because we think something does not mean we have to feel a certain way. We can look at our thoughts critically. Then decide if they should impact how we feel.

For example, you might think, "I made a mistake, so I am a failure." This thought could easily make you feel bad about yourself. But if you really look at the thought, making one mistake does not mean you are a failure. Challenging the thought can help you separate it from the feeling. Then you avoid unnecessary negative feelings.

We need to identify thinking patterns that make us feel bad. By recognizing these patterns, we can reframe our thoughts. This helps neutralize or positively impact our feelings.

Being able to separate thoughts from feelings gives you more control over your emotional well-being. It allows you to interact with the world in a more thoughtful way. Recognizing that thoughts can trigger feelings, but don't have to, lets you choose your emotional reactions carefully. This adds sophistication to your emotional intelligence.

For example, say you are giving an important presentation at work. The thought crosses your mind, "What if I mess up and look incompetent?" This could make you feel nervous and afraid. But instead of accepting that thought, you could challenge it. Is one mistake really proof of incompetence? Does the audience want you to fail? The answer is likely no. Reframing the thought helps avoid unnecessary fear.

Managing feelings is an important part of life. Feelings are personal experiences that come from thoughts, beliefs, and situations around us. When feelings are very strong, we might want to share them with others. But sharing feelings with others can sometimes cause problems, especially if the feelings come more from our own thoughts than from the actual situation.

The key is finding the right balance in sharing feelings. We need to think about when, where, and who to share feelings with to keep relationships healthy and manage our own emotions. Emotional intelligence helps with this. It means understanding our own feelings and being aware of others' feelings too. This helps us decide if it's appropriate to share feelings in a certain case.

If the thoughts behind the feelings come from assumptions, over-generalizations, or unrealistic beliefs, the first step is to examine those thoughts ourselves. If needed, we can ask professionals or trusted people to help us understand these thoughts and feelings better. Their input can give valuable perspective to manage thoughts and feelings more effectively.

Sharing feelings is important for connection and emotional health. But some thoughts that lead to feelings may not connect to the reality of a situation. In those cases, it's best to process those emotions internally before expressing them externally. With self-examination and support, we can learn to transform unhelpful thoughts into constructive thinking patterns. This allows us to share our feelings in a way that builds connections without causing tensions.

Managing your feeling requires tuning into our inner world and the world around us. It takes self-awareness, empathy, and discernment. When feelings overwhelm us, we need spaces for introspection and trusted companions for wise counsel. As we understand the roots of our emotions, we can nurture the ones that reflect reality and transform the ones that distort it. This allows us to express our authentic feelings skillfully and sensitively attuned to others and the context.

Our emotions give colour to our inner landscape. But not all emotions help us see clearly or act rightly. Self-management allows us to filter our feelings wisely so we can share our hearts without causing harm. With care and discernment, we learn when transparent vulnerability nurtures intimacy, and when discretion protects relationships. Emotional intelligence guides us to relate with truth and grace.

Feelings can show our inner state and motivate us. But living only by feelings is risky. Feelings change quickly based on outside events and thoughts. Making long-term choices or usual reactions only by feelings can be inconsistent and lead to regret.

Instead, we need to match our actions and choices to our values, goals, and logical thinking. This doesn't mean ignoring feelings. It means seeing feelings as one thing to think about when living life. Doing this makes a steady framework for acting that is less likely to change with the ups and downs of emotions.

Sometimes feelings that keep coming back can be signs of deeper worries or unsolved problems. When certain feelings keep happening again and again, especially without a clear reason from outside, it's good to look into the thoughts causing these feelings. Are these thoughts based on past experiences, what society expects, or fears without proof? Finding these out can be the first step to solving the worries themselves.

In cases like these, the thoughts and feelings make each other stronger in a loop. Breaking this cycle takes real effort to face the thoughts fueling your worries. Thinking techniques can be very helpful here. They allow you to challenge and reframe the thoughts that bring up the difficult feelings.

Understanding the differences between thoughts and feelings clearly, and knowing how to control feelings, are important steps in achieving emotional balance and wellness. Whether it's telling emotional states and thinking processes apart, or using mindfulness to stop constant worrying, the skills you'll learn from these insights are invaluable life tools.

By recognizing and understanding the differences and connections between thoughts and feelings, we can gain more control over both. This control isn't about ignoring or denying but about managing wisely. Understanding the nature, origins, and impacts of our thoughts lets us live a life guided by thoughtful intention, not ruled by passing emotions.

MASTER *your* FEELINGS

Feelings are the driving force behind every action we take, every decision we make, and every interaction we have. They colour our perceptions, shape our experiences, and influence our behaviour in profound ways. Yet, for many of us, understanding and managing our feelings can become a chore.

Feelings are multifaceted experiences that encompass a range of physiological, cognitive, and behavioural responses. They arise in response to internal and external stimuli, reflecting our thoughts, beliefs, and past experiences. While some feelings, such as joy and contentment, are pleasant and desirable, others, like anger and sadness, may be uncomfortable or distressing. However, feelings serves a purpose, providing valuable information about our needs, desires, and values.

The first step in mastering our feelings is developing awareness of our emotional states. Often, we may find ourselves swept away by intense emotions without fully understanding their origins or implications. By cultivating mindfulness—the practice of nonjudgmental awareness of the present moment—we can observe our thoughts and feelings with clarity and compassion.

As we deepen our awareness of our feelings, we may begin to discern patterns and triggers that shape our responses. Certain situations, memories, or interpersonal dynamics may evoke specific emotional reactions, leading us to behave in predictable ways. By identifying these patterns and exploring their underlying causes, we can gain insight into our emotional tendencies and develop greater control over our feelings. This process of self-discovery requires honesty, curiosity, and a willingness to confront uncomfortable truths.

While we cannot always control the circumstances that elicit our emotions, we can learn to regulate our responses to them. Emotional regulation involves the ability to modulate the intensity and duration of our emotions, allowing us to navigate challenging situations with composure and resilience. Techniques such as deep breathing, progressive muscle relaxation, and cognitive reframing can help us soothe distressing emotions and restore a sense of equilibrium. Additionally, engaging in activities that promote self-care, such as exercise, creative expression, and spending time in nature, can bolster our emotional well-being.

Mastering our feelings also entails cultivating empathy and compassion for ourselves and others. Empathy involves the ability to understand and share the emotions of another person, fostering connection and mutual understanding. By practicing active listening, perspective-taking, and validation, we can deepen our empathy and strengthen our relationships. Likewise, extending compassion toward ourselves— acknowledging our imperfections, forgiving our mistakes, and treating ourselves with kindness—can foster resilience and self-acceptance.

Finally, mastering our feelings requires embracing emotional flexibility—the capacity to adapt and respond effectively to changing circumstances. Rather than rigidly clinging to a single emotional state or response, we can cultivate the flexibility to shift our perspective, reframe challenges as opportunities for growth, and choose how we wish to engage with the world. This willingness to embrace uncertainty and navigate the complexities of human experience with grace and resilience is the hallmark of emotional mastery.

By cultivating awareness, recognizing patterns and triggers, regulating our emotions, nurturing empathy and compassion, and embracing flexibility, we can cultivate emotional intelligence and resilience. Remember, mastering your feelings is not about suppressing or denying your emotions but rather about harnessing their power to live a more authentic, fulfilling life.

In the heart of every soul lies an ocean of emotions, tumultuous and serene, shaping the very essence of who we are. To master these tempestuous waters is to embark on a voyage of self-discovery, navigating the ebbs and flows of joy, sorrow, love, and fear.

Imagine a storm raging within your chest, thundering with anger, quivering with fear, and whispering with sorrow. To master your feelings is to become the captain of your own ship, steering through the tempests of emotion with wisdom and grace. It is not about stifling or suppressing your feelings but rather about understanding them deeply, embracing their nuances, and harnessing their power to propel you forward.

Mastering your feelings began with a journey inward—a pilgrimage to the depths of your own soul. A place where your learn to listen to the whispers of your heart, to honour the sacred wisdom that resides within.

The need to master our feelings is woven into the fabric of our humanity, for emotions are the language of the soul, the currency of connection, and the wellspring of resilience. When we master our feelings, we reclaim agency over our lives, transcending the limitations of circumstance and embracing the fullness of our potential. We forge deeper connections with others, fostering empathy and compassion in the crucible of shared experience. And we cultivate inner peace, anchoring ourselves in the eternal truth of our own worthiness and belonging.

The call to master our feelings echoes through the corridors of time, reverberating in moments of triumph and moments of despair. It beckons to us in the quiet moments of solitude, when the weight of the world rests heavy upon our shoulders, and in the jubilant celebrations of love and connection. It whispers to us in the depths of grief and loss, urging us to find solace amidst the wreckage of shattered dreams. And it guides us through the labyrinth of uncertainty, lighting the way with the flame of courage and resilience.

Emotional mastery knows no bounds, for it is a journey that unfolds in every corner of our lives. It begins within the sanctum of our own hearts, where we tend to the sacred flame of our innermost desires and fears. It extends outward into the world, infusing our relationships with depth and authenticity, and shaping the communities in which we live. And it reverberates across the vast expanse of the cosmos, connecting us to the infinite tapestry of existence.

In truth, the call to master our feelings belongs to each and every one of us—for we are all travellers on the journey of the soul, seekers of truth and bearers of light. It is the artist who channels the raw power of emotion into works of beauty and meaning. It is the healer who holds space for others in their moments of greatest vulnerability. It is the warrior who stands strong in the face of adversity, wielding the sword of courage and resilience. And it is the seeker who embarks on the quest for self-discovery, daring to plumb the depths of their own soul.

Together, we will navigate the stormy seas of emotion, charting a course toward greater self-awareness, connection, and fulfillment. So let us set sail with open hearts and steadfast resolve, for the adventure of a lifetime awaits.

DEVELOP *Mental* TOUGHNESS

Developing mental toughness explores various strategies and techniques to help you cultivate and strengthen your mental resilience. It helps to challenge our emotions, thoughts and feelings when we feel threatened or someone has crossed our boundaries. By embracing these practices, you will be well-equipped to navigate life's challenges and obstacles with a positive mindset and unwavering determination.

Mental toughness is not an innate quality reserved for a select few; instead, it is a skill that can be developed and honed over time. It enables you to face adversity head-on, bounce back from setbacks, and flourish in the face of change. By focusing on the power of your mind, you can unlock the potential within you to overcome obstacles and thrive in all areas of your life.

To better understand mental toughness, we need to explore the mental fortitude that will empower us to thrive in any situation. It will equip us with the tools and knowledge necessary to cultivate a positive and resilient mindset. It will enable us to face challenges head-on and persevere even when the going gets tough.

Remember, developing mental toughness is a continuous process. It requires dedication, practice, and a commitment to personal growth. As we embark on mental toughness, be open to new perspectives and willing to embrace change. With each step you take, you will discover the remarkable strength within you, empowering you to conquer obstacles, achieve your goals, and live a fulfilling life.

One of the critical foundations of mental toughness lies in recognizing and challenging negative self-talk. Our minds have an incredible power to shape our reality, and how we talk to ourselves internally can significantly influence our emotions, behaviours, and overall well-being. We can rewire our brains to transform negative self-talk into positive and empowering affirmations.

Negative self-talk often manifests as self-criticism, doubt, and limiting beliefs that hold us back from reaching our full potential. It is a roadblock to our growth and can significantly impact our confidence and self-esteem. However, by consciously recognizing these negative thought patterns, we can begin the process of rewiring our brains for positive change.

By becoming aware of our negative self-talk, we can challenge and replace these destructive thoughts with more positive and supportive ones. This process involves reframing our perspective and cultivating self-compassion. Instead of criticizing ourselves for perceived shortcomings or failures, we can choose to respond with kindness and understanding.

Through consistent practice and reinforcement of positive messages, it is possible to rewire the brain to believe in one's abilities and potential. These empowering statements become integral to daily life, fostering a solid foundation of self-belief and resilience.

It is essential to approach the journey of rewiring the brain with patience and self-acceptance, as developing mental toughness is gradual. By committing to challenging negative self-talk and embracing positive affirmations, individuals take a significant step towards empowering themselves and creating a more fulfilling life.

Recognizing and challenging negative self-talk unlocks the immense potential within individuals and cultivates a mindset that can overcome any obstacle. We can build a solid foundation of self-belief, resilience, and mental toughness, empowering individuals to thrive in all aspects of life.

Change is an inevitable part of life, and developing mental toughness involves embracing it with a positive and open mindset. We must tap into the transformative power of embracing change and cultivating adaptability and how these qualities can contribute to your mental toughness.

Change provides us with opportunities for growth, self-discovery, and personal development. We open ourselves to new possibilities, experiences, and perspectives by embracing change. Rather than fearing or resisting change, we can choose to see it as a catalyst for progress and transformation.

One of the critical aspects of developing mental toughness is recognizing that change is often accompanied by uncertainty and the unknown. It requires a willingness to step outside our comfort zone and explore uncharted territories. Doing so broadens our horizons and expands our capabilities, fostering personal growth and resilience.

Adaptability goes hand in hand with embracing change. It is the ability to adjust and thrive in different situations, even when circumstances constantly evolve. A mentally tough individual possesses the flexibility and resilience to adapt their mindset, strategies, and actions to meet the demands of a changing environment.

When we cultivate adaptability, we develop a remarkable ability to navigate challenges and setbacks effectively. Instead of becoming overwhelmed or discouraged by unexpected circumstances, we see them as opportunities to learn, evolve, and find creative solutions. This mindset allows us to maintain control and optimism, even when faced with adversity.

Moreover, embracing change and cultivating adaptability

can increase self-confidence and self-belief. As we navigate new experiences and overcome obstacles, we develop a deep-rooted trust in our ability to handle whatever comes our way. This self-assurance becomes a solid foundation for our mental toughness, enabling us to face future challenges with unwavering resolve.

In a world constantly evolving and presenting new challenges, embracing change and cultivating adaptability is a valuable asset. It allows us to thrive in dynamic environments, seize opportunities, and stay ahead of the curve. By fostering these qualities, we position ourselves for success and personal fulfilment.

Embracing change and cultivating adaptability is a process that requires patience and self-reflection. Embrace the unknown with a positive attitude, seek growth opportunities, and trust your ability to adapt and thrive. By doing so, you will develop the mental toughness necessary to navigate life's ever-changing landscape and emerge stronger, wiser, and more resilient.

In the realm of mental toughness, few attributes are as transformative as a growth mindset. A growth mindset is a powerful belief that our abilities and intelligence can be developed and improved through dedication, effort, and a willingness to learn. It is the belief that challenges are growth opportunities, and setbacks are merely stepping stones on the path to success. By cultivating a growth mindset, we open ourselves to a world of possibilities and unleash our true potential.

Embracing a growth mindset is an invitation to view failures not as permanent limitations but as valuable lessons and opportunities for growth. Instead of being discouraged by setbacks, those with a growth mindset approach them with curiosity and resilience. They see obstacles as puzzles to solve and setbacks as temporary roadblocks on the journey toward their goals. They see obstacles as opportunities and failures as fertilizers for their future.

One of the most remarkable aspects of a growth mindset is its ability to reshape how we perceive our abilities and potential. With a growth mindset, we understand that intelligence and talents are not fixed traits but qualities that can be developed over time. This realization liberates us from the constraints of self-imposed limitations and allows us to embrace continuous learning and improvement.

By cultivating a growth mindset, we become more open to taking on challenges outside our comfort zone. We must recognize that stepping into the unknown is an opportunity for personal and professional growth. This willingness to push boundaries and embrace new experiences fosters resilience and adaptability, crucial qualities for navigating life's ever-changing landscape.

Moreover, a growth mindset encourages a positive attitude toward effort and perseverance. Instead of viewing hard work as a burden, individuals with a growth mindset see it as essential to growth and success. They understand that with consistent effort and deliberate practice, they can achieve mastery in any area they choose.

Furthermore, a growth mindset nurtures a love for learning. It encourages a thirst for knowledge, the exploration of new ideas, and a willingness to seek feedback and constructive criticism. This continuous pursuit of education fuels personal and professional growth, propelling individuals toward their goals with unwavering determination.

Cultivating a growth mindset can be developed and strengthened over time. Practice self-compassion and embrace a positive and patient attitude toward your growth. Celebrate your progress and the small victories along the way, for they are stepping stones toward your larger aspirations.

Unlock your true potential, embrace challenges as opportunities for growth, and set out on a path of continuous learning and self-improvement. With a growth mindset as our guiding light, there are no limits to what we can achieve.

Setting realistic goals is a vital component of developing mental toughness. It involves envisioning our desired outcomes and creating a roadmap to achieve them. Setting clear, achievable goals lays the foundation for success and creates a positive mindset that propels us forward.

In achieving our goals, we will inevitably encounter obstacles along the way. These obstacles may come in various forms, such as unexpected setbacks, self-doubt, or external challenges. However, we can overcome these obstacles by cultivating mental toughness and continue moving forward toward our aspirations.

Obstacles are not roadblocks; they are opportunities for growth and learning. With a positive mindset and unwavering determination, we can reframe obstacles as stepping stones to success. Each challenge we encounter serves as a chance to develop resilience, problem-solving skills, and adaptability.

When faced with obstacles, it's essential to approach them with a solution-oriented mindset. Instead of dwelling on the problem, focus on identifying potential solutions and taking proactive steps to overcome them. Embrace the philosophy that every setback is a valuable learning experience, providing insights and knowledge to benefit us in the long run.

Remember, the path to success is rarely a straight line. There will be detours, setbacks, and unexpected hurdles. However, with a positive mindset, realistic goals, and the mental toughness to overcome obstacles, we have the power to navigate these challenges and emerge more robust than ever.

Perseverance, the unwavering determination to keep going despite challenges and setbacks, is a remarkable quality that can propel us toward success and personal growth. There is tremendous power that perseverance holds and how it can contribute to the development of mental toughness in the most positive and uplifting way.

When faced with obstacles and difficulties, it is natural to feel discouraged or tempted to give up. However, by embracing the power of perseverance, we can transform these moments into opportunities for growth and achievement. Through determination, we learn to rise above our circumstances, push our limits, and discover the strength and resilience that lie within us.

One of the critical aspects of developing mental toughness through perseverance is maintaining a positive attitude in the face of adversity. Challenges may seem daunting at first, but cultivating a mindset focused on finding solutions and learning from setbacks can maintain an optimistic outlook even in the toughest of times. With each challenge overcome, our confidence grows, and we become better equipped to face future hurdles.

In today's fast-paced world, stress and anxiety have become increasingly prevalent. However, we view these challenges as opportunities for growth and self-improvement within the realm of developing mental toughness. We can manage stress and anxiety effectively, empowering ourselves to navigate life's pressures with grace and resilience.

It is important to recognize that stress and anxiety are natural responses to the demands and uncertainties of everyday life. They are signals from our bodies and minds, indicating the need for attention and care. Adopting a positive perspective can transform these experiences into catalysts for personal growth, developing the mental toughness needed to thrive in any situation.

Nurturing our physical, emotional, and mental well-being

is crucial for developing mental toughness. Engaging in activities that bring us joy, practicing mindfulness, and prioritizing restful sleep are all integral parts of a self-care routine that can fortify our resilience.

Confidence and self-efficacy are potent attributes that contribute to mental toughness. When we possess a strong sense of confidence, we believe in our abilities and have faith in our capacity to succeed. Self-efficacy, conversely, is the belief in our capability to accomplish specific tasks or goals. Together, they form a dynamic duo that empowers us to overcome challenges and seize opportunities with a positive outlook.

There are various strategies and techniques to help build and bolster our confidence and self-efficacy. By embracing these practices, we will cultivate an unshakable belief in ourselves, enabling us to tackle obstacles and achieve our aspirations with resilience and determination.

Additionally, seeking out new experiences and pushing ourselves beyond our comfort zone can be instrumental in building confidence and self-efficacy. Embrace opportunities that allow us to learn and grow, even if they initially seem daunting. Each new experience provides a chance to prove that we are capable of more than we may have thought originally. With each successful encounter, our confidence will naturally flourish, and our self-efficacy will strengthen.

We must practice self-care and engage in activities that nourish our minds, bodies, and spirits. Taking care of ourselves physically and emotionally contributes to a positive self-image and an enhanced sense of self-worth. Engage in activities that bring us happiness, practice self-compassion, and embrace self-acceptance. The more we prioritize self-care, our confidence and self-efficacy will flourish.

Building confidence and self-efficacy is an ongoing journey requiring patience and perseverance. As we incorporate these strategies into our lives, we will witness a remarkable transformation in how we perceive ourselves and our abilities. With a solid foundation of confidence and self-efficacy, we will approach challenges with resilience, embrace new opportunities, and ultimately achieve our goals with unwavering determination.

In today's fast-paced and increasingly distracted world, focusing and concentrating has become precious skill. Fortunately, it is a skill that can be cultivated and enhanced through dedicated practice and a positive mindset. Some strategies and techniques can help us sharpen our focus and concentration, enabling us to achieve greater productivity and success.

Remember, developing mental toughness is a continuous process. It requires dedication, practice, and a commitment to personal growth. As we move forward, apply the knowledge and insights gained from this chapter in our daily lives. Let's embrace the challenges that come our way as opportunities for growth and learning. Let's celebrate our progress, no matter how small, and be patient with ourselves during setbacks.

Developing mental toughness is not about achieving perfection or never experiencing difficulties. It's about building the resilience and inner strength needed to overcome obstacles, bounce back from setbacks, and thrive amidst the uncertainties of life. It's about developing a mindset that sees challenges as stepping stones to growth and transformation. It's about rewiring our brains.

Let's carry the wisdom and practices gained. Let's embrace the power of our minds, trust in our abilities, and believe in our capacity to face any challenge that comes our way. With mental toughness, we possess the inner strength to persevere, the resilience to bounce back, and the unwavering determination to achieve our goals and live a fulfilling life. We have facts and reasons to validate our feelings and what we think. We should have confidence, resilience, and a renewed sense of purpose. We can embrace mental toughness, knowing that we have the strength within us to overcome anything that comes our way.

POSITIVE MINDSET

The power of a positive mindset is undeniable. It shapes our perceptions, influences our emotions, and fuels our actions to shape of feelings and what we think. When we embrace positivity, we open ourselves to a world of possibilities, where obstacles become opportunities and setbacks transform into stepping stones towards personal growth and success. However, maintaining a positive mindset requires conscious effort and a commitment to self-improvement regardless of how we feel and what we think.

Embracing optimism as a way of life must be a central theme to reduce stress and anxiety and allow the past to float away from our present. It's the key to embrace our feelings and what we think from abuse, traumas, addictions, toxic relationships, a negative past, regrets, mistakes, and wrong doing.

Adopting an optimistic mindset can positively impact our lives, relationships, and overall happiness. By shifting our perspective and focusing on the possibilities and potential inherent in every situation, we can create a life infused with hope, resilience, and a deep appreciation for the journey.

Sustaining a positive mindset requires consistent practice. We need practical tips and strategies to incorporate into our daily routines, ensuring positivity becomes a habit rather than a fleeting state of mind. By nurturing our minds and conditioning ourselves to stay positive, we can lay the foundation for a lifetime of happiness and fulfillment.

A positive mindset is a powerful tool that can significantly impact our lives and world experience. It is the foundation upon which we build our thoughts, emotions, and actions, shaping our perceptions and influencing our overall well-being. Understanding the power of a positive mindset requires recognizing its profound effects on various aspects of our lives. It will enable us to approach challenges and obstacles with resilience and optimism. Instead of being overwhelmed by difficulties, we will view them as opportunities for growth and learning. It is our ability to find solutions and persevere that increases our chances of overcoming obstacles and achieving success.

Moreover, a positive mindset enhances our emotional well-being. When we adopt a positive outlook, we tend to experience more positive emotions, such as joy, gratitude, and contentment. These positive emotions have a ripple effect, influencing our overall mood and improving our mental and emotional state. By focusing on the positive aspects of our lives, we can counteract negative emotions and cultivate a sense of well-being.

A positive mindset enhances our relationships and social interactions. When we approach others with positivity, we radiate warmth and kindness, creating a positive environment that fosters more profound connections. Our positive attitude attracts like-minded individuals and strengthens existing relationships. By maintaining an optimistic perspective, we can build and nurture meaningful connections that enrich our lives.

Furthermore, a positive mindset can improve our physical health. It can positively impact our immune system, cardiovascular health, and overall well-being. When we maintain a positive mindset, we are more likely to engage in healthy behaviours such as regular exercise, a balanced diet, and adequate rest, all of which contribute to better physical health.

Additionally, a positive mindset opens us up to a world of possibilities. When we believe in ourselves and our abilities, we are more willing to take risks, explore new opportunities, and step outside our comfort zones. This mindset encourages us to embrace change, seize opportunities, and pursue our goals and dreams with enthusiasm and determination. By cultivating a positive mindset, we expand our horizons and create a fulfilling life aligned with our aspirations.

Understanding the power of a positive mindset requires acknowledging that it is not about denying or ignoring the challenges and hardships of life. Instead, it is about choosing to focus on the positive aspects, finding meaning in adversity, and responding to difficulties with resilience and optimism. A positive mindset empowers us to shape our reality and create a life that is filled with happiness, fulfillment, and a deep appreciation for the present moment.

The science behind conditioning the mind for positivity is rooted in the fields of neuroscience, psychology, and cognitive behavioural therapy. These disciplines provide valuable insights into how our thoughts, emotions, and behaviours are interconnected, offering a framework for understanding and harnessing the power of a positive mindset.

A positive mindset is an ever-present force, weaving its threads through the fabric of our existence. Having a positive mindset is not always easy; it requires us to let go of familiar patterns and step into the unknown. Yet, within this dance of transformation lies immense power and potential for personal growth.

Picture yourself standing on the precipice of change, looking into the vast horizon of possibilities. It may be a desire to break free from unhealthy habits, explore new passions, or embark on a journey of self-discovery. Whatever the catalyst, embracing change is about shifting our perspective and adopting a growth mindset.

A positive mindset is the belief that our abilities,

intelligence, and talents can be developed through dedication, effort, and learning. It is a mindset that sees challenges as opportunities for growth, setbacks as stepping stones to success, and obstacles as invitations to push beyond our comfort zones. By embracing this mindset, we open ourselves up to the transformative power of change.

Change begins with self-reflection and a deep understanding of our desires and aspirations. Take a moment to listen to the whispers of your heart, to uncover the yearnings that have been tucked away amidst the demands of daily life. What dreams have you postponed? What passions have you neglected? Embrace change by acknowledging these desires and committing to pursue them with unwavering determination.

A positive mindset often challenges our sense of identity and disrupts the familiar patterns that have provided comfort and security. It's natural to feel a sense of unease or fear as you step outside your comfort zone. However, personal growth lies just beyond the boundaries of familiarity. Embrace change by acknowledging these fears but refusing to let them dictate your path. Channel your energy towards building resilience and cultivating the courage to move forward.

A positive mindset is not a linear process but rather a series of small steps and moments of transformation. Break down your goals into manageable tasks and celebrate each milestone along the way. Acknowledge that progress may be accompanied by setbacks and hurdles. Embrace change by viewing these challenges as opportunities for self-reflection, learning, and adaptation. Every stumble becomes an invaluable lesson that propels you further along your journey.

Seek out new experiences, broaden your horizons, and explore uncharted territories. Embrace change by embracing curiosity, open-mindedness, and a willingness to learn. Step outside your comfort zone, whether trying a new hobby, learning a new skill, or connecting with different cultures and perspectives. Embrace change by seeing every encounter as an opportunity for growth, expanding your understanding of the world and yourself.

Embrace a positive mindset with open arms, for it is through change that we evolve, learn, and become the best version of ourselves. Adopt a growth mindset, view challenges as stepping stones, and honour the call of your innermost desires. Embrace change, for within its embrace lies the transformative power that will shape your journey toward personal growth and fulfilment.

Reframing negative experiences involves finding empowering and constructive perspectives when faced with adversity or setbacks. It is about shifting our mindset and looking for alternative ways to interpret challenging situations. One approach is to look for lessons or opportunities for growth within the adversity. Consider what you can learn from the experience or how it can contribute to your personal development. By reframing setbacks as valuable learning experiences, you can extract wisdom and find motivation to keep moving forward.

We need to focus on the potential for positive outcomes or silver linings. We could ask ourselves, "What good can come out of this situation?" or "How can I turn this setback into an opportunity?" We can cultivate a more optimistic and resilient mindset by identifying and embracing the potential benefits.

We need to consider the bigger picture and how the negative experience fits into the context of our life's journey. Sometimes, setbacks can redirect us towards paths more aligned with our goals and aspirations. Reflect on whether the setback might guide you towards a different and potentially better path.

We need to challenge any self-limiting beliefs that arise from negative experiences. Instead of viewing setbacks as evidence of personal failure or inadequacy, recognize that they are a normal part of life and do not define your worth or abilities. Reframe the experience as an opportunity to challenge and overcome obstacles, reinforcing your resilience and inner strength.

A positive mindset involves finding empowering and constructive perspectives when faced with adversity or setbacks. It is about shifting our mindset and looking for alternative ways to interpret challenging situations. One approach is to look for lessons or opportunities for growth within the adversity. Consider what you can learn from the experience or how it can contribute to your personal development. By reframing setbacks as valuable learning experiences, you can extract wisdom and find motivation to keep moving forward.

We need to focus on the potential for positive outcomes or silver linings. We could ask ourselves, "What good can come out of this situation?" or "How can I turn this setback into an opportunity?" We can cultivate a more optimistic and resilient mindset by identifying and embracing the potential benefits.

We need to consider the bigger picture and how the negative experience fits into the context of our life's journey. Sometimes, setbacks can redirect us towards paths more aligned with our goals and aspirations. Reflect on whether the setback might guide you towards a different and potentially better path.

We need to challenge any self-limiting beliefs that arise from negative experiences. Instead of viewing setbacks as evidence of personal failure or inadequacy, recognize that they are a normal part of life and do not define your worth or abilities. Reframe the experience as an opportunity to challenge and overcome obstacles, reinforcing your resilience and inner strength.

We should explore cultivating gratitude, which involves fostering a mindset that focuses on the positive aspects of life and appreciating the things we often take for granted. By practicing gratitude, we can shift our perspective from lacking or negative to what we have and the positive experiences we encounter.

Shift your focus from what's missing to what's present. Often, we tend to focus on what we lack or what went wrong. Instead, consciously redirect your attention to the abundance in your life. Acknowledge the positive experiences, relationships, and opportunities you have been blessed with.

When facing challenges or setbacks, try to find silver linings or lessons within them. Reflect on how difficult experiences have shaped you, taught you resilience, or provided new insights. Shifting your perspective to see the growth potential in adversity can foster a sense of gratitude for the lessons learned.

Practice a positive mindset. Recognize and appreciate your strengths, accomplishments, and efforts. Celebrate your progress and the steps you have taken toward personal growth. Treat yourself with kindness and acknowledge your value and worth.

Engage in acts of kindness and service. Giving back to others can cultivate a sense of gratitude and fulfilment. Volunteer your time, lend a helping hand, or engage in random acts of kindness. By extending kindness to others, you not only make a positive impact on their lives but also deepen your sense of gratitude.

Remember that a positive mindset is a practice that requires consistent effort and mindfulness. It may not always come naturally, especially during challenging times. Still, by intentionally cultivating gratitude, you can shift your focus toward the positive aspects of life, foster a sense of appreciation, and enhance your overall well-being.

We need to take the time to observe our feelings, thoughts, emotions, and reactions without judgment. Notice the times when we are being self-critical or harsh towards ourselves. This awareness is the first step towards practicing self-compassion.

A positive mindset challenge and reframe self-critical thoughts. When we notice self-critical thoughts arising, we must ask ourselves if we would say the same things to a friend in a similar situation. Often, the answer is no. Learn to treat yourself with the same kindness and understanding you would offer someone else. Reframe negative self-talk into more compassionate and supportive language.

A positive mindset incorporates self-care regularly. Engage in activities that nurture your physical, emotional, spiritual and mental well-being. This can include exercise, healthy eating, getting enough rest, engaging in hobbies you enjoy, and seeking support from loved ones. Prioritize self-care as an essential part of your life.

Cultivate a non-judgmental attitude towards your mistakes and failures. Understand that making mistakes is a natural part of growth and learning. Treat yourself with understanding and kindness when things don't go as planned. Instead of dwelling on the past, focus on what you can learn from the experience and how to grow from it.

A positive mindset involves engaging in positive self-talk,

which is also very important to consider in challenging negative thoughts which can lead to negative behaviours. It consists in harnessing the power of positive affirmations and consciously reframing our thoughts and beliefs. It is about intentionally cultivating a more optimistic and supportive inner dialogue.

We need to start by becoming aware of our inner critic. Notice the negative thoughts or self-limiting beliefs that arise in our minds. We must consider how these thoughts make us feel and impact our self-esteem and confidence.

Once we have identified negative self-talk patterns, challenge them with positive affirmations. Affirmations are positive statements that reflect the reality we want to create or the qualities we want to embody. We must repeat these affirmations to ourselves regularly, with conviction and belief. For example, if you struggle with self-doubt, you can affirm, "I am capable and deserving of success."

Reframe negative thoughts into more positive and constructive ones. Whenever a negative thought arises, we can consciously challenge it by asking ourselves if there's an alternative, more empowering perspective. For example, if you catch yourself thinking, "I always mess things up," reframe it as "I am learning and growing from every experience."

We need to practice self-compassion in our self-talk. Treat ourselves with kindness, understanding, and patience. Instead of berating ourselves for mistakes or perceived shortcomings, offer encouragement and support. We must remind ourselves that making mistakes is a natural part of learning and that we deserve love and compassion.

We need to be mindful of the language we use when talking to ourselves while maintaining a positive mindset. We should be choosing words that are uplifting, empowering, and supportive. We should avoid using negative or harsh language that reinforces self-doubt or self-criticism. Let's cultivate a positive and nurturing tone in our self-talk.

Visualization also can be a powerful tool to enhance positive self-talk. We can create mental images of ourselves succeeding, achieving our goals, and embodying the qualities we aspire to have. As we visualize, we can reinforce these images with positive affirmations. This practice helps us "Embrace Imperfections" and align our thoughts with a more positive self-perception.

We must surround ourselves with positive influences and seek individuals, books, or resources to inspire and uplift us. We must engage in conversations or activities that foster positivity and encourage self-belief. Surrounding ourselves with positive influences can support and reinforce our positive self-talk.

Consistency is critical when it comes to engaging in positive self-talk. Make it a habit to practice positive affirmations and reframe negative thoughts consistently. Over time, with this practice, we can "Embrace Imperfections" to naturally lean towards positive self-talk and foster a more optimistic and empowering mindset.

Remember that engaging in positive self-talk is a process that requires effort and mindfulness. It may take time to shift deeply ingrained patterns of negative self-talk, but with persistence and patience, you can cultivate a more positive and supportive inner dialogue. We can enhance our self-esteem, confidence, and overall well-being by harnessing the power of positive self-talk.

A positive mindset can be considered another outlet to challenge our negative thoughts and behaviours. It involves prioritizing activities that nurture our mental and emotional well-being, promoting a positive outlook and overall sense of balance in life. It is about intentionally setting aside time and energy to care for ourselves.

We need to recognize the importance of a positive mindset and the impact it has on our mental and psychological well-being. Understand that being positive is not selfish but necessary for overall health and happiness. Embrace the belief that you deserve to prioritize your needs and engage in activities that bring you joy and rejuvenation.

We need to identify activities that replenish and energize us. A positive mindset can take many forms, unique to each individual. It could be engaging in hobbies you love, spending time in nature, practicing mindfulness or meditation, reading a book, taking a relaxing bath, or simply enjoying quality time with loved ones. Discover what activities bring you a sense of peace, fulfilment, and relaxation.

We can create self-care as a means of a positive mindset routine. Set aside dedicated time each day or week for self-care activities. We must treat these moments as non-negotiable and prioritize them in our schedule. We should consider them as essential appointments with ourselves. This routine can help us establish a healthy balance and ensure that self-care becomes a consistent practice.

Nurturing our physical well-being through self-care is essential. We need to exercise regularly, prioritize healthy eating habits, get enough sleep, and listen to our body's needs. Taking care of our physical health contributes to our overall well-being and promotes a positive outlook.

We need to set boundaries and learn to say no. Prioritizing our own needs and learning to say no to commitments or requests that may overwhelm us or drain our energy. Creating healthy boundaries allows us to protect our time and energy, giving us more space for self-care activities.

We should practice self-compassion as part of our self-care routine and treat ourselves with kindness and understanding. We need to accept that we are not perfect and that it is okay to have limitations or make mistakes. We must embrace self-compassion in moments of difficulty or self-criticism, offering ourselves words of love and encouragement.

We should regularly reassess and adjust our self-care routine as needed. Our needs and circumstances may change over time, so it's essential to periodically evaluate our self-care practices and adapt accordingly. We need to listen to our intuition and be open to exploring new activities or approaches to self-care that resonate with us.

We must remember that a positive mindset is not a luxury but a necessity. By prioritizing positive mindset activities, we can invest in our mental and emotional well-being, promoting a positive outlook and a healthier relationship with ourselves and others. We should embrace a positive mindset as an ongoing practice supporting our overall happiness and fulfilment.

Let us embrace the idea that setbacks and obstacles are a natural part of growth. If we encounter challenges or temporarily veer off track, we can offer ourselves understanding and kindness. Use these moments as opportunities to learn, adjust, and recommit to our goals with renewed determination.

Our quest for self-mastery can continue as we engage in deep self-reflection. Through journaling and introspection, we can venture into the depths of our psyche, unravelling the underlying motivations behind our impulsive behaviour. This introspective journey serves as a compass, illuminating the path to lasting change.

With emotional regulation skills as our steadfast companions, we can equip ourselves with practical strategies to manage and regulate our emotions. These invaluable tools will allow us to navigate the stormy seas of life with grace and composure, reducing the likelihood of impulsive reactions that may hinder our progress.

Patience can become our ally as we embrace the art of delayed gratification. We can hone our ability to resist immediate temptations in favour of long-term benefits and personal growth. Through this practice, we can sow the seeds of discipline and fortitude, nurturing a resilient spirit that withstands the allure of impulsive choices.

We can harness the power of positive reinforcement to reinforce our commitment and dedication. By implementing techniques that reward and reinforce desired behaviours, we can lay a solid foundation for lasting change. We can discover the joy of celebrating small victories, cultivating a sense of accomplishment and motivation that propels us forward.

As we approach the culmination of our transformative journey, we craft a structured action plan—a roadmap that redirects our impulsive tendencies toward healthier alternatives. With a clear direction and unwavering resolve, we navigate the complexities of life, charting a course that aligns with our most authentic aspirations.

We can revel in the beauty of self-control, and as we celebrate those moments, no matter how small, we exercise restraint and demonstrate self-control. In these triumphs, we can find the fuel to propel us further along the path of self-discovery and growth, knowing that we possess the strength and resilience to conquer our impulsive impulses.

With each step we take each lesson we learn, we move closer to a life guided by intention and empowered choice. Let us embark on this journey together, embracing the transformation that awaits us as we learn to stop ourselves and step into a brighter future.

To gain control over a positive mindset, the first crucial step is to become keenly aware of the triggers that set off a chain reaction of impulsive or destructive behaviours within us. These triggers can take various forms, ranging from external circumstances to internal thoughts and emotions. By closely examining and identifying these triggers, we empower ourselves to intervene before they hijack our rationality and steer us off course.

A positive mindset is often tied to specific situations or environments that provoke impulsive reactions. For some, it might be the sight of a particular substance or object that triggers an irresistible craving. Others might find themselves vulnerable to impulsive behaviours when faced with social pressures or specific social settings. By paying attention to the external factors that consistently elicit impulsive responses, we can proactively devise strategies to navigate these triggers more effectively.

Equally significant are the internal triggers that reside within our thoughts and emotions. Negative self-talk, self-doubt, or feelings of inadequacy can be potent catalysts for impulsive actions. Similarly, intense emotions such as anger, sadness, or stress can overwhelm our rational thinking, leading us down a path of impulsive behaviour. By honing our self-awareness, we can detect the subtle cues that indicate the presence of these internal triggers, allowing us to intercept and disrupt their influence.

A positive mindset is essential to engage in a process of honest introspection and reflection. This may involve keeping a journal or diary to document instances when we find ourselves giving in to impulsivity. By reviewing these entries, patterns may emerge, providing valuable insights into the triggers that consistently precede impulsive behaviours. Additionally, seeking guidance from therapists, counsellors, or support groups can offer an outside perspective and help shed light on triggers that might be less apparent to us.

In this exploration, it is essential to approach the process without judgment or self-criticism. Recognizing triggers is not about placing blame or labelling ourselves negatively; instead, it is a compassionate and empowering act of self-discovery. By understanding the circumstances, thoughts, or emotions that ignite our impulsive tendencies, we gain the power to choose a different course of action.

A positive mindset is crucial to remain patient and persistent. Triggers may not always be immediately apparent; uncovering them may require time and reflection. It is a process of peeling back the layers of our experiences and emotions to reveal the root causes of our impulsive behaviours.

Ultimately, by recognizing a need for a positive mindset, we gain the ability to anticipate and intercept impulsive urges before they escalate. Armed with this knowledge, we can develop personalized strategies and coping mechanisms to navigate these triggers more effectively. By taking control of our responses and breaking the automatic cycle of impulsivity, we pave the way for healthier and more intentional choices, leading us towards a life of greater fulfilment and well-being.

A positive mindset profoundly impacts our thoughts, behaviours, and overall well-being. They possess the power to propel us toward impulsive actions or guide us toward thoughtful and deliberate choices. We need to develop our emotional intelligence as a critical skill to master.

At its core, emotional intelligence is the ability to recognize, understand, and manage our own emotions and the emotions of others. It encompasses a range of competencies, including self-awareness, self-regulation, empathy, and effective communication. By honing these skills, we equip ourselves with the tools to navigate the tumultuous terrain of intense emotions and prevent them from driving us toward impulsive actions.

The first step in harnessing emotional intelligence is cultivating self-awareness. It involves developing a deep understanding of our emotions, recognizing their triggers, and acknowledging how they influence our thoughts and behaviours. This heightened self-awareness allows us to catch ourselves in the grip of intense emotions before they propel us toward impulsive reactions.

It is the art of managing our intense emotions; we can respond thoughtfully and effectively rather than reacting impulsively. Self-regulation involves recognizing and acknowledging our emotions without being overwhelmed by them. We can learn to pause, take a step back, and consciously choose our responses, even in the face of intense emotional storms. This practice enables us to regain control over our actions and make decisions aligned with our long-term goals and values.

A positive mindset is a crucial element of emotional intelligence that supports our journey towards stopping impulsive behaviours. Empathy involves the ability to understand and share the feelings of others. By developing empathy, we cultivate a deeper understanding of the perspectives, needs, and emotions of those around us. This understanding helps us navigate interpersonal relationships with compassion and sensitivity, reducing the likelihood of impulsive reactions driven by misunderstandings or unchecked emotions.

Effective communication is an essential skill that complements a positive mindset. It involves expressing our emotions and needs in a clear and constructive manner while also being receptive to the feelings and needs of others. By honing our communication skills, we create an environment that encourages open dialogue, understanding, and collaborative problem-solving. This fosters healthier interactions and reduces the likelihood of impulsive outbursts or miscommunications that can lead to regrettable actions.

As we develop a positive mindset, it is essential to remember that it is a lifelong journey. It requires patience, practice, and a willingness to learn and grow continually. By investing time and effort into developing emotional intelligence, we lay the foundation for a more balanced and mindful approach to managing intense emotions. We gain the ability to recognize the warning signs of impulsivity and to choose responses that align with our values and long-term well-being.

Harnessing a positive mindset is a powerful tool to stop ourselves from succumbing to impulsive actions. By developing self-awareness, self-regulation, empathy, and effective communication, we gain the capacity to understand and manage intense emotions that can drive impulsive behaviours. With a positive mindset as our guide, we navigate the complex landscape of emotions with grace and intention, forging a path toward a more fulfilling and purposeful life.

In pursuing a positive mindset, positive reinforcement emerges as a powerful tool to reshape our behaviours and strengthen our resolve. By understanding the principles of positive reinforcement and implementing them in our lives, we can pave the way for lasting change and growth.

A positive mindset involves the deliberate use of rewards or incentives to encourage and reinforce desired behaviours. It operates on the premise that when a behaviour is followed by a positive consequence, such as a reward or recognition, the likelihood of that behaviour being repeated in the future increases. In essence, we train our minds to associate the desired behaviour with pleasurable outcomes, motivating us to continue making conscious choices.

One effective technique in utilizing a positive mindset is to identify and define specific behaviours that align with our goals and values. By clearly defining what constitutes a desired behaviour, we create a tangible target to aim for. This clarity enables us to recognize and appreciate our progress and make adjustments.

We must identify meaningful and personalized rewards that resonate with us to implement a positive mindset. These rewards can take various forms, such as treats or indulgences, quality time with loved ones, engaging in a favourite hobby, or even acknowledging our achievements through self-affirmation. The key is to select rewards that are personally meaningful and serve as incentives for us to stay on track.

Consistency is paramount when utilizing a positive mindset. By consistently and promptly providing rewards for desired behaviours, we reinforce the connection between our actions and the positive outcomes they bring. This consistency strengthens the neural pathways in our brains, making it easier for us to choose the desired behaviours over impulsive actions in the future.

In addition to immediate rewards, we can also implement delayed or cumulative reinforcement. Delayed reinforcement involves rewarding ourselves after successfully maintaining desired behaviours over a certain period. This approach helps us develop patience and the ability to delay gratification, which is essential for long-term personal growth.

A positive mindset involves tracking and celebrating our progress over time and accumulating rewards for consistent effort and improvement. This technique allows us to acknowledge and appreciate the incremental steps we take on our journey, reinforcing our commitment to change.

It is important to note that a positive mindset should not be seen as a means of punishment or judgment for our past impulsive actions. Instead, it is a compassionate and empowering approach that focuses on acknowledging and nurturing the positive changes we make in the present. By shifting our focus to the desired behaviours we want to reinforce, we create a supportive and growth-oriented environment within ourselves.

As we implement a positive mindset, we gradually "Embrace Imperfections" and cultivate a mindset that embraces conscious choices and self-control. We learn to associate the rewards and positive outcomes with the behaviours that serve our higher goals and aspirations. Over time, these reinforced behaviours can become ingrained in our daily lives, replacing impulsive actions with intentional, mindful decision-making.

In pursuing a positive mindset, by rewiring the brain, creating an action plan becomes an indispensable tool on our transformative journey. An action plan serves as a roadmap, guiding us towards healthier alternatives and redirecting our impulsive tendencies onto a path of growth and self-improvement.

We lay the groundwork for a focused and effective action plan by clearly identifying the impulsive tendencies that hinder our progress. This clarity allows us to target our efforts and channel our energy toward the areas that require our attention the most. We need first to define our goals and aspirations. We may want to ask ourselves, "What are the specific behaviours we seek to change?"

Once we have identified our goals, it is essential to break them down into smaller, manageable steps. This step-by-step approach enables us to progress incrementally, providing a sense of accomplishment and motivation. By setting realistic and achievable milestones, we cultivate a sense of empowerment and build momentum towards lasting change.

In developing a positive mindset, it is vital to explore and research alternative behaviours that align with our desired outcomes. What healthier choices can we make when faced with impulsive urges? Are there specific strategies or coping mechanisms that resonate with our values and strengths? When we explore these possibilities, we expand our repertoire of options and arm ourselves with the tools needed to navigate challenging moments.

Accountability plays a crucial role in the effectiveness of a positive mindset. We may seek support from trusted friends, family members, or professionals who can provide guidance and hold us accountable for our commitments. Sharing our intentions and progress with others creates a network of support and encouragement, bolstering our motivation and providing valuable feedback.

As we implement a positive mindset, it is essential to remain flexible and adaptable. We may encounter setbacks or obstacles that test our resolve. In these moments, we must be willing to reassess our strategies, make necessary adjustments, and learn from our experiences. Embracing a positive mindset allows us to view setbacks as opportunities for growth and development, reinforcing our determination to succeed.

Regular evaluation and reflection are integral components of a positive mindset. By periodically assessing our progress, we can celebrate the milestones achieved, acknowledge areas for improvement, and refine our approach as needed. Self-reflection provides insights into our patterns and triggers, allowing us to make informed choices and further refine our action plans.

Throughout this process, it is crucial to cultivate self-compassion and kindness towards ourselves. A positive mindset is a journey that requires patience and understanding. It is natural to encounter moments of difficulty or relapse. By treating ourselves with compassion and refraining from self-judgment, we create a nurturing environment for growth and increase our resilience in the face of challenges while developing a positive mindset.

Celebrating the achievements and moments of a positive mindset becomes an essential part of our action plan. Every small victory, no matter how seemingly insignificant, deserves recognition. By acknowledging and celebrating our progress, we reinforce positive behaviours and boost our confidence, fuelling our motivation to continue on the path of self-improvement.

In creating a positive mindset to redirect impulsive tendencies towards healthier alternatives, we lay the foundation for transformative change. By deliberately cultivating new habits and choices, we reclaim our power and forge a path toward a more balanced and fulfilling life. We need to be determined resilient, and carry an unwavering commitment to a positive mindset

Sustaining positive change begins with a deep-rooted commitment to yourself. Recognize the significance of your progress and reaffirm your dedication to a healthier and more fulfilling life. Embrace the belief that you can maintain this positive trajectory and deserve the happiness and well-being that come with it.

We must develop strategies to support our long-term success with a positive mindset. We must reflect on the practices and routines that have helped us share our self-destructive habits thus far. Identify the triggers and temptations that can pull us back into old patterns and devise strategies to mitigate their influence. This could involve creating a supportive environment, surrounding ourselves with positive influences, and establishing boundaries to protect our progress.

We should establish healthy habits as a solid framework to sustain a positive mindset. Consistency is vital, as it solidifies new behaviours and minimizes the likelihood of slipping back into old patterns. We should integrate these habits into our daily routine, making them a non-negotiable part of our lives. Whether it's dedicating time to exercise, preparing nutritious meals, practicing mindfulness, or seeking moments of self-care, commit to these habits wholeheartedly.

Find joy in the journey. Sustaining a positive mindset is not just about maintaining discipline; it's about embracing the beauty of the process itself. Celebrate the small victories, relish in the progress you continue to make, and savour the moments of growth and self-discovery along the way. Cultivate gratitude for the opportunity to transform your life and let it fuel your determination to stay the course.

As discussed earlier, we must embrace a growth mindset that views challenges as opportunities for learning and growth. Recognize that setbacks are a natural part of any journey and see them as stepping stones rather than roadblocks. When faced with obstacles, assess them objectively, extract the lessons they hold, and use them to further refine your strategies for sustaining positive change.

Above all, be kind and patient with yourself. Recognize that maintaining a positive mindset is a lifelong commitment, and there may be times when you stumble or falter. Embrace these moments as opportunities for growth and self-compassion. Learn to forgive yourself, recalibrate, and recommit to your journey. Remember that every day is a fresh start—a chance to reaffirm your dedication and continue the legacy of positive change you have begun.

A positive mindset is an ever-present force, weaving its threads through the fabric of our existence. Embracing a positive mindset is not always easy; it requires letting go of familiar patterns and stepping into the unknown. Yet, within this dance of transformation lies immense power and potential for personal growth.

Picture yourself standing on the precipice of change, looking into the vast horizon of possibilities. It may be a desire to break free from unhealthy habits, explore new passions, or embark on a journey of self-discovery. Whatever the catalyst, embracing change is about shifting our perspective and adopting a growth mindset.

A positive mindset is the belief that our abilities, intelligence, and talents can be developed through dedication, effort, and learning. It is a mindset that sees challenges as opportunities for growth, setbacks as stepping stones to success, and obstacles as invitations to push beyond our comfort zones. By embracing this mindset, we open ourselves up to the transformative power of change.

A positive mindset begins with self-reflection and a deep understanding of our desires and aspirations. Take a moment to listen to the whispers of your heart, to uncover the yearnings that have been tucked away amidst the demands of daily life. What dreams have you postponed? What passions have you neglected? Embrace change by acknowledging these desires and committing to pursue them with unwavering determination.

As you embark on this journey, be prepared to encounter resistance. A positive mindset often challenges our sense of identity and disrupts the familiar patterns that have provided comfort and security. It's natural to feel a sense of unease or fear as you step outside your comfort zone. However, personal growth lies just beyond the boundaries of familiarity. Embrace a positive mindset by acknowledging these fears but refusing to let them dictate your path. Channel your energy towards building resilience and cultivating the courage to move forward.

A positive mindset is not a linear process but rather a series of small steps and moments of transformation. Break down your goals into manageable tasks and celebrate each milestone along the way. Acknowledge that progress may be accompanied by setbacks and hurdles. Embrace a positive mindset by viewing these challenges as opportunities for self-reflection, learning, and adaptation. Every stumble becomes an invaluable lesson that propels you further along your journey.

Seek out new experiences, broaden your horizons, and explore uncharted territories. Embrace a positive mindset by embracing curiosity, open-mindedness, and a willingness to learn. Step outside your comfort zone, whether trying a new hobby, learning a new skill, or connecting with different cultures and perspectives. Embrace a positive mindset by seeing every encounter as an opportunity for growth, expanding your understanding of the world and yourself.

Embrace a positive mindset with open arms, for it is through change that we evolve, learn, and become the best version of ourselves. Adopt a growth mindset, view challenges as stepping stones, and honour the call of your innermost desires. Embrace a positive mindset, for within its embrace lies the transformative power that will shape your journey toward personal growth and fulfilment.

DEVELOP POSITIVITY

Developing positivity becomes invaluable in a world filled with challenges, uncertainties, and negativity. It is a mindset that allows individuals to navigate life's ups and downs with grace, resilience, and a sense of empowerment. It helps to embrace feelings that may be impacted by negativity. The benefits of cultivating positivity extend beyond just feeling good; they have a profound impact on our mental and physical well-being, as well as on our relationships and overall outlook on life.

Developing positivity and its transformative effects can significantly impact our lives, how we think and feel. The power of optimism has ways in which a positive mindset can shape our perception of the world. Additionally, the science behind positivity, examining its impact on brain chemistry and how it can rewire our thought patterns, helps us to see "the light at the end of every dark tunnel."

Practicing gratitude and appreciation are essential tools for nurturing positivity. By learning to acknowledge and cherish the blessings, big and small, in our lives, we can foster a sense of contentment and joy that radiates throughout our days. Moreover, the power of positive affirmations and how they can reshape our self-perception, boost self-confidence, and invite positive change into our lives have proven effective in maintaining calmness and peace within our hearts and minds.

Negativity bias, a common tendency to focus on the negative aspects of life, can hinder our progress in cultivating positivity. We can overcome this bias and reframe our thinking, allowing ourselves to embrace a more positive and balanced perspective.

Surrounding ourselves with positive influences is another crucial aspect, as the people and environments we engage with significantly impact our mindset and overall well-being.

We must find joy in our everyday life. By cultivating mindfulness and seeking out moments of beauty and inspiration, we can enhance our appreciation for the present moment and infuse our days with happiness and purpose.

Additionally, self-compassion and kindness foster positivity, as treating ourselves with love and understanding is key to developing a healthy and resilient mindset.

Building resilience through positive thinking is an essential skill to overcome adversity and bounce back from setbacks. We uncover strategies to cultivate resilience and embrace a growth mindset by enabling ourselves to approach challenges with optimism and find valuable lessons within them.

The ripple effect of spreading positivity to others and how our own positive mindset can inspire and uplift those around us creates a harmonious and supportive social environment.

By developing positivity, we open ourselves to a world of possibilities, experiencing profound benefits to our overall well-being, relationships, and outlook on life. There is the transformative power of cultivating positivity and unlocking our extraordinary potential.

Developing and maintaining a positive mindset is essential for overall well-being and can profoundly impact various aspects of life. A positive mindset is characterized by optimism, hope, and the belief that one can overcome challenges and achieve success.

Our thoughts and beliefs shape our perception of the world and influence our emotions, actions, and overall outlook on life. A positive mindset involves consciously focusing on the positive aspects of situations, people, and experiences rather than dwelling on the negative. By recognizing and challenging negative thoughts and replacing them with positive ones, we can reframe our perspective and develop a more optimistic outlook.

A positive mindset has a direct impact on mental and emotional well-being. Optimistic individuals tend to experience lower levels of stress, anxiety, and depression. They are better equipped to cope with challenges, setbacks, and adversities as they approach them with resilience, perseverance, and a belief in their ability to overcome obstacles. This resilience helps to reduce the impact of adverse events and promotes psychological well-being.

A positive mindset fosters a proactive and solution-oriented approach to problem-solving. When faced with challenges or setbacks, a positive mindset are more likely to view them as opportunities for growth and learning rather than insurmountable obstacles. This mindset allows for greater creativity, flexibility, and the ability to generate effective solutions, leading to increased productivity and success in various endeavours.

Positivity is contagious. A positive mindset tends to attract and maintain healthier relationships and social connections. An optimistic outlook and positive energy can uplift others, create a harmonious atmosphere, and foster deeper connections. By cultivating positivity, we can become more empathetic, compassionate, and supportive, strengthening interpersonal relationships and contributing to overall social well-being.

A positive mindset fuels motivation and perseverance, making setting and pursuing goals easier. When faced with setbacks or obstacles, a positive attitude maintains a belief and the ability to focus on the possibilities for success. This determination and resilience increase the likelihood of achieving personal and professional goals, leading to a greater sense of fulfilment and satisfaction.

By actively adopting these strategies, we can develop a positive mindset and unlock its numerous benefits in all areas of life. The power of optimism lies in its ability to transform perspectives, enhance well-being, and create a brighter and more fulfilling future.

Developing a positive mindset goes beyond simply thinking positively; it also involves understanding the science behind positivity and how it affects our brain chemistry.

When we experience positive emotions such as happiness, gratitude, or love, our brain undergoes specific changes that contribute to our overall well-being. One of the key players in this process is the neurotransmitter dopamine, often referred to as the "feel-good" chemical. Dopamine is associated with feelings of pleasure, motivation, and reward. When we engage in activities that evoke positive emotions, such as spending time with loved ones or pursuing hobbies, our brain releases dopamine, creating a sense of satisfaction and contentment.

Moreover, positive emotions have been found to activate the prefrontal cortex, the part of the brain responsible for executive functions like decision-making, planning, and problem-solving. This activation enhances our cognitive abilities, improves our ability to focus, and boosts our overall mental performance.

Positive emotions also contribute to the growth of new neural connections and promote neuroplasticity, which is the brain's ability to adapt and change throughout life. This means that by regularly experiencing positive emotions, we can literally rewire our brains to become more receptive to positivity and improve our overall mental well-being.

In addition to the immediate effects on brain chemistry, cultivating positive feelings over time has numerous long-term benefits. Positive emotions have also been linked to improved cardiovascular health, more substantial immune function, and a longer lifespan.

Furthermore, the science of feelings reveals the concept of emotional contagion, which suggests that our emotions can be contagious and influence the emotional states of those around us. When we radiate positivity, it can have a ripple effect, spreading to others and creating a more positive and supportive social environment. This underscores the importance of cultivating positivity not only for our personal well-being but also for the well-being of those around us.

Understanding the science behind feelings can be a powerful motivator for incorporating positive practices into our daily lives. By actively seeking out positive experiences, engaging in activities that bring us joy, and consciously focusing on gratitude and appreciation, we can harness the transformative power of positivity and create a virtuous cycle of well-being and happiness.

Understanding the connection between feelings and brain function gives us valuable insights into how positivity can enhance our overall well-being, improve cognitive abilities, promote physical health, and foster positive social interactions. Armed with this knowledge, we can make informed choices and actively work towards developing a more positive mindset, ultimately leading to a more fulfilling and happier life.

Positive feelings are powerful statements that help shift our mood from negative to positive. They are a tool to rewire our thoughts and beliefs, fostering a more optimistic and empowered outlook. We can harness our transformative power and experience numerous benefits by consciously and consistently practicing positive affirmations.

Positive feelings work by influencing our subconscious mind, which is responsible for shaping our beliefs, attitudes, and behaviours. When we repeat affirmations, we overwrite negative thought patterns and replace them with positive and empowering ones. This rewiring process helps us adopt a more positive mindset over time.

Feelings are particularly effective in boosting self-confidence and self-esteem. By affirming positive qualities and capabilities within ourselves, we build a stronger sense of self-worth and belief in our abilities. This increased self-confidence can lead to tremendous success and fulfilment in various areas of our lives.

Positive feelings can strengthen our resilience in the face of adversity. We develop a more positive outlook during challenging times by reminding ourselves of our inner strengths, stability, and ability to overcome obstacles. Feelings can help us stay focused, motivated, and persistent, enabling us to navigate challenges easily.

Feelings play a crucial role in cultivating a positive mindset. By consistently repeating positive statements, we train our minds to focus on the positive aspects of life. This shift in perspective enables us to approach situations with optimism, see opportunities in challenges, and maintain a hopeful outlook.

Positive feelings can significantly enhance motivation and drive toward achieving our goals. By affirming our abilities to succeed, our commitment to our purposes, and our beliefs in ourselves, we strengthen our resolve skills and determination. This increased motivation propels us forward, helping us overcome obstacles and achieve our desired outcomes.

Feelings have a positive impact on our emotional well-being. By consistently repeating uplifting statements, we create a more positive emotional state. Feelings can help reduce stress, anxiety, and negative emotions by replacing them with feelings of calm, confidence, and optimism. This improved emotional state contributes to overall well-being and happiness.

Positive feelings can also strengthen our relationships with others. When we cultivate a positive mindset and use feelings that promote kindness, compassion, and understanding, we approach our interactions with a more positive attitude. This positivity can foster better communication, deeper connections, and more harmonious relationships.

To harness the power of positive feelings effectively, we need to phrase our thoughts in a specific and positive manner as if the desired outcome is already happening. For example, say, "I am confident and capable in everything I do."

Visualize and feel the positive outcome as you repeat your feelings. Engaging your senses helps create a more vivid and compelling experience, reinforcing positive beliefs. Tailor your commitments to align with your specific goals, values, and aspirations. Customizing feelings makes them more meaningful and relevant to your journey.

By incorporating positive feelings into your daily routine and embracing their power, you can transform your mindset, enhance your well-being, and unlock your full potential for a more positive and fulfilling life.

It's common to encounter situations that trigger negative emotions, feelings or thoughts daily. This negativity bias, a natural tendency of the human mind, can overshadow positive experiences and hinder personal growth. However, by understanding and overcoming this bias, we can actively foster positivity and improve our overall well-being.

Negative bias refers to the tendency to give more weight and attention to negative information compared to positive information. This bias is deeply rooted in our evolutionary history, where our ancestors needed to prioritize potential threats for survival. While this bias served a purpose in the past, it can be detrimental in today's world, where adverse events and emotions often dominate our attention.

Developing awareness and consciously reframing our thoughts and feelings to foster positivity and overcome negative bias is crucial. One effective strategy is cognitive restructuring, which involves identifying and challenging negative thoughts and replacing them with more positive and realistic ones. We can gradually rewire our thinking patterns by questioning the validity of negative beliefs and actively seeking evidence to support positive alternatives.

Furthermore, practicing self-compassion is essential in overcoming negative bias. It involves treating ourselves with kindness, understanding, and acceptance, especially in the face of setbacks or self-criticism. Acknowledging and validating our emotions can create a supportive internal dialogue that counteracts negative bias and fosters self-growth.

In addition to our efforts, creating a positive environment supporting our journey toward positivity is important. Surrounding ourselves with positive influences, such as uplifting and supportive friends, family, or communities, can profoundly impact our mindset. These positive connections provide a network of encouragement, motivation, and inspiration, which can help us overcome negativity and foster a more positive outlook on life.

By actively working to overcome negative bias and foster positivity, we can experience a range of benefits. Improved mental and emotional well-being, increased resilience, and enhanced overall life satisfaction are some of the rewards of cultivating positivity. Moreover, fostering positivity benefits us individually and creates a ripple effect, influencing those around us in a positive way. We project positivity through our feelings and how we process information.

By actively challenging negative thoughts, cultivating mindfulness, practicing self-compassion, and surrounding ourselves with positive influences, we can break free from the limitations of negativity bias. Embracing positivity allows us to experience greater happiness, resilience, and fulfilment while also spreading the seeds of positivity to others.

Surrounding ourselves with positive influences is essential to developing and maintaining a positive mindset. The people and environments we expose ourselves to significantly impact our thoughts, emotions, and well-being. By consciously choosing to surround ourselves with positivity, we can enhance our positive outlook and increase our chances of leading a happier and more fulfilling life.

One of the first steps in surrounding yourself with positive influences is to evaluate the relationships in your life. Consider the people you spend the most time with and reflect on how they make you feel. Do they uplift and inspire you? Do they radiate positivity and encourage personal growth? Surrounding yourself with individuals who embody these qualities can be incredibly empowering. Optimistic people tend to exude optimism, offer support during challenging times, and provide constructive feedback when needed. Their positive energy can be contagious, motivating you to adopt a similar mindset and outlook.

Creating an environment that aligns with your values and promotes positivity can profoundly impact your well-being. Consider adding elements that bring you joy, such as vibrant colours, meaningful artwork, plants, or natural light.

It's important to acknowledge that not all life influences will always be positive. Challenges, setbacks, and negative experiences are inevitable. However, by consciously surrounding yourself with positive influences, you can build resilience and develop strategies to navigate challenging times with optimism and strength. Positive influences can serve as a source of encouragement, reminding you of your potential and inspiring you to overcome obstacles.

Surrounding yourself with positive influences is a powerful strategy for cultivating and maintaining a positive mindset. Evaluating and nurturing your relationships, creating uplifting environments, curating positive media consumption, and engaging with supportive communities are all ways to surround yourself with positivity.

By actively seeking out these influences, you can enhance your overall well-being, build resilience, and increase your capacity for joy and personal growth. Remember, positivity is contagious, and by surrounding yourself with positive influences, you benefit yourself and contribute to creating a more positive and uplifting world for others.

Finding joy in everyday life involves a conscious shift in perspective and a willingness to appreciate the beauty and goodness in even the simplest of moments. It's about embracing the present moment and fully engaging with the experiences and people around us. Doing so can enhance our overall sense of happiness and contentment.

By regularly reflecting on what we are grateful for, we shift our focus away from what may be lacking or challenging and redirect it toward what is going well. This shift in perspective can help us find joy in the abundance surrounding us, fostering a greater sense of contentment and happiness.

Engaging in activities that bring us joy is essential for finding happiness in everyday life. These activities can vary significantly from person to person and might include hobbies, creative pursuits, spending time in nature, or connecting with loved ones. By consciously making time for activities that bring us joy, we prioritize our well-being and create opportunities for moments of happiness to flourish.

By actively reframing negative thoughts and focusing on the positive aspects of any given situation, we empower ourselves to seek out and appreciate the moments of joy that exist amidst challenges. Developing resilience and an optimistic outlook can help us gracefully navigate life's ups and downs and find joy even in the face of adversity.

Positivity has a remarkable ripple effect, spreading its influence far beyond the individual who cultivates it. When we embrace a positive mindset and actively practice positivity, we can profoundly impact those around us, creating a domino effect of happiness, inspiration, and resilience.

One of the key ways in which positivity spreads to others is through social contagion. As negativity and stress can be contagious, positivity can also be infectious. Radiating positive energy and engaging in optimistic behaviours can inspire and uplift those in our social circles. Our enthusiasm, kindness, and optimism can influence others to adopt a more positive outlook on life.

Positivity can create a supportive and nurturing environment. When we choose to focus on the good in others, offer encouragement, and celebrate their successes, we develop a sense of belonging and affirmation. This, in turn, enhances their well-being and empowers them to embrace positivity in their own lives. The supportive atmosphere we foster encourages personal growth, resilience, and a willingness to take on challenges.

Furthermore, by spreading positivity, we become role models for others. Our actions and words carry weight, and when we consistently demonstrate a positive mindset, we inspire others to follow suit. People look up to those who radiate optimism and happiness, and they are more likely to adopt similar attitudes and behaviours. By being an agent of positive change, we can motivate and empower others to make positive changes and contribute to a collective culture of positivity.

Positivity spreads to others through acts of kindness and compassion. When we extend a helping hand, show empathy, or engage in small acts of generosity, we create a ripple effect of positivity. These acts uplift us and inspire others to pay it forward, creating a chain reaction of positivity that can touch countless lives.

Moreover, spreading positivity to others has reciprocal benefits. When we uplift others, we experience a sense of fulfilment and purpose. Witnessing our positive impact on someone's life fuels our positivity and motivates us to continue spreading joy and kindness. This reciprocal relationship between positivity and its propagation serves as a reinforcement, continually strengthening our commitment to positivity and expanding its reach.

Developing positivity is a transformative journey that benefits individuals and society tremendously. By cultivating a positive mindset and embracing optimism, we can shape our perspectives and approach life's challenges with resilience and hope. The science of positivity reveals its profound impact on brain chemistry, reinforcing that our thoughts and emotions can shape our neural pathways and overall well-being.

Overcoming negative bias and fostering positivity requires conscious effort and self-awareness. By recognizing our ingrained tendencies, we can challenge and replace negative thoughts, cultivating a more optimistic and constructive mindset. Surrounding ourselves with positive influences through supportive relationships or inspiring content can further fuel our journey toward positivity.

Building resilience through positive thinking enables us to bounce back from setbacks and face adversity with strength and determination. By nurturing our mental and emotional stability, we become better equipped to navigate life's challenges and emerge stronger than before.

Spreading positivity to others holds immeasurable value. We can inspire and uplift those around us through our words, actions, and demeanour, creating a supportive and optimistic environment. The ripple effect of our positivity has the potential to touch countless lives, fostering a collective sense of hope, compassion, and joy.

Developing positivity is a lifelong journey that requires commitment, self-reflection, and consistent practice. By embracing the power of optimism, gratitude, kindness, and resilience, we unlock our potential to "Rewire Your Brain," which leads to a fulfilling life and makes a meaningful impact on the world. Our efforts to cultivate positivity will benefit us and create a brighter and more harmonious future for all.

CONCLUSION

As we reach the conclusion of our journey, we reflect on the profound insights gained from our exploration of thoughts, mastering our feelings, developing mental toughness, and cultivating a positive mindset. Throughout this transformative odyssey, we have uncovered the undeniable power of our thoughts and their influence on our emotional experiences.

We have we learned to recognize the pivotal role our feelings and thoughts play in shaping our emotions. By mastering our thoughts, we gain control over our feelings and pave the way for greater emotional resilience and well-being.

In the pursuit of mental toughness, we embraced challenges as opportunities for growth and transformation. By developing resilience and grit, we fortified ourselves against adversity and emerged stronger and more resilient than ever before.

Throughout our journey, we cultivated a positive mindset, anchoring ourselves in optimism, gratitude, and self-belief. Through the power of positive thinking and affirmations, we rewired our brains for positivity and abundance, embracing life's possibilities with unwavering confidence and optimism.

As we bid farewell to this journey, let us carry forth the lessons learned, and the wisdom gained into our daily lives. May we continue to harness the power of our thoughts, master our feelings, develop mental toughness, and cultivate a positive mindset in every aspect of our lives. With each step forward, may we embody resilience, optimism, and unwavering faith in our ability to overcome any obstacle and achieve our highest aspirations. Together, let us embrace the journey of self-discovery and personal growth with open hearts and boundless optimism.

We have learned that mastering our feelings is a crucial aspect of personal growth and well-being for several compelling reasons. It empowers us to navigate life's challenges with resilience and composure. Inevitably, we encounter obstacles and setbacks on our journey, but by mastering our emotions, we can respond to these challenges with clarity and effectiveness. Rather than being overwhelmed by negative emotions such as fear or anxiety, we can approach difficulties with a sense of calmness and determination, enabling us to overcome adversity more effectively.

Secondly, mastering our feelings enhances our relationships with others. Emotions play a significant role in our interactions with friends, family, colleagues, and acquaintances. When we are unable to regulate our emotions, we may react impulsively or lash out in moments of stress, damaging our relationships and causing unnecessary conflicts. By mastering our feelings, we can communicate more effectively, empathize with others, and build stronger, more meaningful connections.

Furthermore, we have learned that mastering our feelings promotes mental and emotional well-being. Unmanaged emotions such as chronic stress, anger, or sadness can take a toll on our mental health, leading to anxiety, depression, and other psychological issues. When we learn to regulate our emotions, we reduce the negative impact of stress on our bodies and minds, leading to greater overall well-being and resilience.

Moreover, mastering our feelings fosters personal growth and self-awareness. By understanding and managing our emotions, we gain insight into our own thought patterns, beliefs, and behaviors. This self-awareness enables us to identify areas for improvement, break free from destructive habits, and cultivate healthier, more adaptive coping strategies.

In essence, mastering our feelings is essential for leading a fulfilling and balanced life. It empowers us to navigate life's challenges with resilience, enhances our relationships with others, promotes mental and emotional well-being, and fosters personal growth and self-awareness. By developing the ability to regulate our emotions effectively, we can create a life characterized by greater peace, fulfillment, and success.